Introduction

This paper focuses on why France, a country with tremendous advantages in resources and military strength, was defeated by a group of poorly equipped and largely untrained Algerian insurgents who mainly operated in groups of ten to twenty men and probably never had over fifteen thousand active fighters inside the borders of Algeria.[1] France failed to understand the nature of the war and why the Algerians were fighting. This failure led the French to misidentify the Algerian strategic center of gravity and by their actions, to make French centers of gravity, their legitimacy to rule and their will to fight, vulnerable to attack. This paper will illustrate this by analyzing French and Algerian will, intelligence, and civil-military relations.

The Algerian War of Independence began early on the morning of November 1, 1954, when Algerian insurgents launched a series of loosely coordinated guerilla attacks[2] that left seven victims dead and four wounded.[3] This paper's analysis will begin at the Philippville massacre of August, 1955, which marked an escalation of Algerian insurgent ferocity and resulted in a formerly reformist French Governor-General's taking a much sterner line in the prosecution of the conflict. What followed was a staggeringly long low-intensity conflict that lasted until President Charles de Gaulle proclaimed Algerian independence on July 3, 1962, ending France's 120-year colonial empire in the Maghreb.[4]

The Algerian insurrection merits investigation because France seized the military initiative after three years of war. By the start of the fifth year, the French had largely driven the enemy from the field of battle and believed themselves to be on the cusp of victory. Just over two years later, however, they were withdrawing in defeat. The Defense Department's Directorate for Special Operations and Low-Intensity Conflict has held screenings of the film

"Battle of Algiers" to glean lessons from the French experience in Algeria.[5] The enduring

nature of the Global War on Terror virtually ensures that the United States will be involved in

similar low-intensity conflicts in the future. Critical to winning these contests is an

understanding of the nature of the war and lessons from the past that may provide valuable

perspective for the future. This paper will provide background historical information, analyze

the conflict, reach conclusions, and offer recommendations for the future.

Background

French influence in Algeria dates from the Middle Ages. Trade between France and

North Africa was burgeoning in the thirteenth century.[6] By the eighteenth century France had

begun to monopolize trade with North Africa.[7] While a comprehensive review of events

between then and the outbreak of the Algerian insurrection is outside the scope of this paper,

discussion of a few key events and groups that form the basis for the conflict is necessary to

provide historical context.

Colonial Conquest: Until the nineteenth century, France had better relations with

Algiers than her European or American contemporaries.[8] However, prolonged negotiations

over a debt to Algerian merchants, incurred by Napoleon's armies in Egypt, caused relations

between Algiers and Paris to sour and, by 1827, to become a crisis.[9] In response to an insult

against the French consul in Algiers, the French King Charles X undertook an escalating

series of military actions resulting in the May 25, 1830 invasion in which 635 ships set sail for

Algiers with thirty-four thousand troops aboard.[10] By July 5, the invaders had defeated a

force of seven thousand Turks, seventeen thousand Kabyles (Berbers), and nineteen thousand

additional troops from Constantine and Oran.[11] Despite arriving in Algeria proclaiming that their mission was to liberate the people residing there from the Turks,[12] the French conquest was unusually violent.[13].

Fierce resistance to the invasion continued in remote regions until 1857 by which time France had extended its control from the coastal cities to all of the land north of the Sahara desert.[14] France annexed the conquered territories and considered them to be a part of the *metropole,* integral to France, rather than simply a colonial possession.[15]

Colons: Often referred to disparagingly as *pied-noirs,* the *colons* were European settlers in Algeria. Although initially of French descent, by 1917 eighty percent of the *colons* were of other nationalities, mainly Spanish and Italian.[16] The *pied-noirs* were largely middle and lower middle class artisans, fishermen, and laborers[17] and, by 1954, they numbered approximately one million.[18] These one million Europeans collectively owned ninety percent of industry and forty percent of the most fertile land.[19] Distribution of wealth among the *colons* was far from equitable, however. Two percent of the farmers, the *grand-colons,* owned twenty-five percent of the land[20] while the poorest ten thousand, the *petit-blancs,* were hardly better off than their Muslim contemporaries.[21] Regardless of national origin or social position, the *colons* identified with metropolitan France and were largely indifferent to the poverty of native Algerians, who they considered subhuman.[22]

Muslims: The Muslim population consisted of two distinct ethnic groups. The Kabyles (Berbers) were the original inhabitants of Algeria who were forcibly converted to Islam by invading Arabs in the seventh century[23] and were the largest ethnic group.[24] Most had intermarried with Arabs while the approximately one third who remained ethnically distinct resided primarily in the remote mountain regions.[25] Arabs and Arabized Berbers resided in the coastal regions , owned small farms and businesses, and had the most contact with the French, which was not entirely positive. The majority of *colon* land expansion came at the expense of this group.[26]

As a result of improvements in medical care provided by the French the Muslim population expanded dramatically from five million in 1926 to 8.5 million in 1954.[27] Under French rule, the literacy rate had dropped from forty percent in 1830[28] to approximately ten percent in 1954.[29] In 1954 Muslim unemployment was twenty-five percent.[30] Following the colonial conquest, French government institutions replaced Ottoman institutions.[31] Colonization devastated the Arab aristocracy. Most Arabs sustained themselves on ever-shrinking farms or to abandoned their land and moved to city slums.[32]

Islamic Reform Movement: Algeria's reform movement began in the 1920s and was inspired by Egyptian reformers.[33] The reformers focused on religious purification and allegiance to the Arab community rather than to France.[34] In 1936, movement leader Ben Badis wrote that in his examination of history he had discovered a "Muslim Algerian nation" and that "this Algerian nation is not France, cannot be France, and does not wish to be France".[35] Although its support was focused in the Constantine area, Muslim masses responded favorably to the movement.[36]

French Army: The French Army sought to regain its pride following losses in 1940 at the hands of the Germans, and in 1954, in Indochina. Numbering 56,500 in Algeria in 1954,[37] the Army's mission was to protect the one million *colons*.[38] Defeat in Indochina had left the officer corps distrustful of their chain of command and feeling betrayed by their government.[39]

Politics: Although the French claimed the three Algerian departments were integral parts of metropolitan France, an appointed governor-general (normally a colonial position) administered Algeria.[40] Reforms instituted in 1919 gave Muslims, who made up ninety percent of the population, the right to elect half of the members of the Algerian assembly. Europeans elected the other fifty percent. A two-thirds majority was required to pass most important bills giving the *colons* power greatly exceeding their numbers.[41] Other reforms allowed certain elite Algerians, mainly veterans of French Army service or those educated in France, to become French citizens. This privilege came at a cost of renouncing certain rights such as the right to trial under Islamic law and, as a result, very few Algerians availed themselves of this opportunity.[42]

Thousands of Algerians fought on the French side during the World War I and many who did not fight took the place of French soldiers in the factories of France.[43] Exposure to Wilsonian ideals and a higher standard of living highlighted the vast gulf between life in Algeria and the principles for which France claimed to stand. A small number of Muslim students were chosen to be educated with European students to fill the role of interlocutors between the French administrators and Muslim masses.[44] Students enrolled in these schools were taught French, not Arab, history. One consequence was these students gained exposure to the ideals of the Enlightenment and the French Revolution, ideals that were to influence greatly the movement towards national liberation.[45]

During World War II, Algerian Muslims generally sided with the French despite the fact that, under the Vichy government, they lost some of their hard won progress towards equality.[46] Following the liberation of North Africa, Algerians offered to fight on the side of the Free French if they were permitted to hold a Muslim assembly to develop their own institutions "within an essentially French framework".[47] This request was denied and the French offered only insufficient versions of old reforms that had been rejected by the *colons*.

Failure to offer more substantive reforms resulted in a shift away from more moderate parties such as Ferhat Abass's *Union Democratique du Manisfeste* (UDMA) party towards Messali Haj's militantly nationalist *Mouvement pur la Triomphe des Liebertes Democratiques* (MTLD).[48] The MTLD formed a secret organization, the *Organization Speciale* (OS) to prepare for armed revolution.[49] The OS was discovered and broken up by French police, but Ben Bella, one of the leaders of the MTLD formed a new secret organization with a similar purpose, the *Comite Revolutionnaire d'Unite et d'Action* (CRUA).

Eventually the CRUA renamed itself the *Front de Liberation Nationale* (FLN) and took the role of political leadership of the Algerian War of Independence.[50] The FLN located itself in Cairo and was headed by a nine-member council. The military wing of the FLN, the *Armee de Liberation Nationale* (ALN) took responsibility for fighting the war inside of Algeria, which they divided into six provinces, *Wilayas*, each headed by an ALN colonel. These six colonels made up the interior leadership of the war effort.[51] The FLN and ALN remained unknown to the French and began to organize their four hundred mujahadeen for military action.[52] The result was the November 1, 1954 uprising.

Analysis

Desired End States, Objectives, and Centers of Gravity: France's desired end state was to maintain Algeria as an integral part of France. Premier Mendes-France expressed French opinion following the November 1 1954 uprising: "The Algerian departments are part of the French Republic... Between them and metropolitan France there can be no conceivable secession".[53] This point of view was opposed by the FLN and other nationalist parties, although there was debate on whether their goal should be complete independence or some type of Algerian home rule while remaining federated with France. If the average Algerian

Muslim supported independence in November of 1954, it does not appear that he was willing to use violent means to achieve it.

Surprised by the November attacks, the government of Premier Mendes-France backed away from planned reforms. Despite his bellicose and populist speech, Mendes-France realized that the political status quo in Algeria was not sustainable.[54] The French initially believed that the uprising was lawlessness and adopted a program of repression to identify those who carried out the attacks. The Minister of the Interior, Francois Mitterand, sought to limit the amount of force used in the operation and prohibited the use of napalm and shelling of villages.[55] The French identified the Algerian center of gravity as the insurgent leadership. The French operational objective was to eliminate that leadership in order to institute reforms from a position of strength.

The Algerian insurgents realized that their small force, armed mainly with hunting rifles, would be unable to defeat the French in open battle. They sought to wage war in the Maoist mode of protracted insurgency. Hit-and-run attacks and terror bombings would undermine the legitimacy of the French government while motivating the large Muslim population to join with the ALN against the French. In the ALN's view, the French strategic center of gravity was their will to fight for French Algeria. The ALN's operational objective was to attack and weaken the French Army in order to break the French will to hold Algeria.

Philippeville Massacre: After ten months of fighting, the Muslim population of Algeria had not risen to join the FLN in fighting for their freedom. The French responded to the November uprising by arresting MTLD members and conducting a series of raids using NATO-style forces in large armored columns to seek decisive battle with the insurgents. The

French continued to treat the struggle as an internal matter and used censorship to keep it hidden from worldwide scrutiny.[56]

The FLN sought to provoke harsh French reprisals which would mobilize the population to support their efforts and eliminate rivals. On August 20, 1955, demonstrators, organized by ALN mujahadeen, started riots in the mining town of Philippeville and nearby villages.[57] Contrary to their earlier practice of not targeting European civilians, the ALN inspired mobs carried out brutal massacres, killing men, women, and children alike. The victims ranged from "a seventy-three-year old grandmother to a five-day-old baby".[58] Also targeted were anti-FLN Muslims including Abbas Aloua, nephew of Ferhat Abbas, a political rival to the FLN leadership. All told, the mobs killed 123, including seventy-one Europeans.[59]

The French response was immediate and harsh. By the count of the government, the French "forces of order" killed 1273 in response to the Philippeville massacre. A later FLN investigation claimed over twelve thousand deaths, a figure which was never disproven.[60] Other results of the French response included a declaration, by Muslim moderates in the Algerian assembly, that condemned the French policies of blind repression and collective punishment and rejected integration with France. The declaration virtually eliminated any chance of Muslim acceptance of Governor General Jacques Soustelle's proposed reforms.[61]

The events at Philippville transformed Soustelle from a committed integrationist reformer to a hard-liner.[62] Soustelle launched a two-pronged attack against the ALN. In order to combat the ALN hold on the remote areas of the interior he directed the CINC, General Lorillot, to reorganize the Army to face the challenges of lightly armed insurgents. The result was a shift from heavy armored columns to a system of *quadrillage* in which small teams of soldiers garrisoned remote population centers augmented by mobile pursuit forces.[63] The garrison forces were supported by twenty-six thousand indigenous troops known as *harkis*, chosen for their ability to provide intelligence on the local populace and knowledge of terrain.[64] Additionally, the French expanded the *Sections Administratives Specialisees* (SAS) whose mission was to solve the problem of "under-administration" in the large remote areas populated only be Muslims.[65] Small teams of soldiers provided education, agricultural improvements, and health care to people who had little exposure to French government and culture.[66] In order to provide the necessary manpower for *quadrillage* a stop-loss program was instituted and sixty thousand reservists were recalled.[67]

What does this mean with respect to understanding the nature of war? First, French will remained strong. There was little departure from the party line of "French Algeria". A failure to understand the shift in Algerian attitudes towards independence gave the ALN time to establish itself in the countryside. French intelligence improved following the arrest of MTLD members and the incorporation of the native *harkis* into the anti-insurgent effort. Concerning propaganda however, the French policies of collective repression and the use of heavy firepower against villages had largely undermined their credibility as "forces of order". Regular Army forces' indiscriminate use of firepower could undermine months of SAS success at building relationships with Muslims in seconds. While stories of French brutality had not made it into the world media, the indiscriminate use of force combined with ALN terror against Muslims who collaborated with the Europeans undermined the French theater-strategic center of gravity, their legitimacy to govern in the eyes of the governed.

FLN/ALN Actions: The FLN/ALN realized that they could not inflict significant damage upon the French Army. In August of 1956, the leadership of the FLN and ALN held a conference in the Soummam Valley to more distinctly define their objectives, to provide a formal structure to the ALN, and to establish conditions for war termination.[68] In Algeria the ALN was to weaken the French forces enough to prevent a military victory.[69] Internationally the FLN was to "seek out maximum, material, moral, and psychological support" and "incite the intervention of the UN".[70] The conditions for war termination included FLN primacy at any negotiations, recognition of the 1956 Algerian borders, and a prohibition of dual citizenship for any Europeans who chose to remain in Algeria.[71] In order to carry out the two missions of weakening the French militarily and isolating and undermining them internationally, the leadership decided upon a terror offensive in Algeria and an effort to seek support abroad.

Terror Campaign: The purpose of the ALN terror campaign was twofold. First was the desire to establish the FLN as the sole authority over the Muslim population. In Algiers bombings were used to eliminate rival organizations.[72] In September of 1956, the terror campaign in Algiers began in earnest when three teenage girls, chosen specifically because they were not likely to be searched by the French, planted bombs in three heavily trafficked areas of the capital.[73] In late December, Amedee Froger, the mayor of Algiers and a *colon* sympathizer, was assassinated by the ALN. Other bombings targeted mainly at civilians continued through the spring.

Besides wreaking havoc in Algiers, the bombings showed that the ALN was alive and well to the rural population, which was under the net of *quadrillage.* Any positive military effect was short lived however, as Robert Lacoste, the Algerian governor-general, ordered the Tenth Parachute Division under General Massu to take charge of all law enforcement in Algiers and restore order by any means necessary.[74] The paratroopers took to their work with a vengeance. They broke a planned eight-day strike, timed to coincide with United Nations discussions on Algeria, in only two days.[75] Adapting the strategy of *quadrillage* to the Casbah, Algiers' teeming slum of Muslims, the paratroopers cordoned off the area block by block, checked identification, and organized a type of neighborhood watch system to discourage terrorists.[76] Police files were seized and suspected nationalists rounded up without regard to civil law. Interrogation methods were harsh and the Army used torture to gain intelligence on the insurgents' organization.

The ALN leadership council fled to the newly independent Tunisia and, of the two ALN tactical commanders of the Battle of Algiers, Saadi Yacef surrendered to French paratroopers and Ali la Pointe committed suicide to avoid capture.[77] The opening of the Battle of Algiers marked the high point for ALN operations in Algeria. From this time on, all of the nationalist victories would come in the political realm.

International Recognition: The FLN first achieved international recognition at the Bandung conference of Third World nations in April of 1955.[78] International recognition became increasingly important to the FLN as it became evident that the ALN would not be able to defeat the French by military means alone. In September of 1958, the FLN formed an Algerian government in exile, the Provisional Government of the Republic of Algeria (GPRA). Pakistan, Communist China, and the Arab league quickly recognized the government.[79] With money and arms from these governments, the GPRA built a ten-thousand-man army in Tunisia. This force was isolated from Algeria by the Morice Line of border fortifications, but added weight to GPRA legitimacy claims. The GPRA also consolidated its control over Algerian workers in France, adding yet another source of funds to its coffers.[80] Finally, the GPRA rigidly held to the war termination objectives established at the Soummam Conference when tentative negotiations began with de Gaulle's government in 1959. De Gaulle sought a negotiating partner who were more malleable, but outside of an abortive attempt with a single ALN Wilaya commander, none was forthcoming.[81]

Result: The nationalists shared a cultural heritage that stemmed from the Islamic revival and over a hundred years of harsh and inequitable French rule. This united them in achieving their goal of evicting the French from Algeria. By capitalizing on French blunders by means of propaganda and establishing a government in exile and an army in being, they were able to erode the will of the French despite achieving little military success.

French Reaction: After the initial surprise of the November 1, 1954 attacks, the French attempted to regain the initiative. While they were successful at the operational level, an inordinate focus on military accomplishments led them to commit several blunders that placed them on the strategic defensive. By not understanding why the Algerians sought independence, the French were unable to answer adequately the insurgents' challenge to their leadership.

Propaganda: Blunders and harsh military tactics exposed the French to unwanted international attention. Because the French considered Algeria an integral part of the *metropole*, they sought to exclude international bodies from interfering in French internal affairs. The French undermined that claim and drew unwanted international attention to events in Algeria by their seizure of FLN leader Ben Bella aboard a Moroccan jet. Acting on intelligence, the military ordered the French captain of the Moroccan plane, escorted by fighters, to land in Algiers where the French took Bella into custody. Premier Mollet had disapproved the mission, but the military went ahead with it in defiance.[82] The capture attracted harsh international criticism and eliminated any chance of negotiations between Mollet and the FLN.[83]

The combined French and British operations to capture the Suez Canal, launched on November 5, 1965, soon diverted international attention from the Bella capture. The British feared that the Egyptian President, Gamel Nasser, was on a course to become the next Hitler while the French sought to sever the supply of weapons from Nasser's Egypt to the ALN.[84] Instead the combined diplomatic pressure of the United States and the Soviet Union forced the British and French to withdraw. The result was a morale boost for ALN guerillas, while France was politically separated from her most powerful ally, the United States. French soldiers who took part in the Suez mission felt that their government had cheated them of a victory.[85]

French tactics inside Algeria were no less of a propaganda liability. During the Battle of Algiers, the use of torture to obtain intelligence was widespread. As many as three thousand prisoners "disappeared" from French custody during the Battle of Algiers.[86] Written accounts of this activity, such as Servan-Schreiber's 1958 *Lieutenant in Algeria* and Henri Alleg's *La Question*, began to appear in France resulting in the growth of an anti-war bloc.[87] Torture, forced resettlement of villagers, and broken promises of reform did little to endear the Muslim population to continued rule by the French, discredited French claims to legitimacy in Algeria, and isolated France from her allies.

Civil-Military Relations: After winning a tactical victory in the Battle of Algiers and conducting successful follow on operations, the Army believed that victory was within its grasp. Some commanders called for military control of the government, both in Algeria and France, in order to achieve total victory.[88] Instead, they were faced with a new government, reportedly prone to compromise with the FLN, which caused the French Army to fear that they would be betrayed yet again by their civilian leaders.[89] Seizing upon unrest in the capital, the Army, under General Massu, took power in Algiers and an invasion of Paris seemed imminent.[90] The threat of a coup achieved the result that the *colons* and the Army sought – the return to power of General de Gaulle June 1, 1958.[91]

The Army and certain retired senior officers worked with extremist *colons* to threaten the civilian government two more times when they disagreed with governmental objectives. The first was in January of 1960, during the "Barricades Week", when the Army refused to fire on a *pied-noir* mob that was protesting de Gaulles' offer of self-determination to Algeria and killed several police officers attempting to disperse them.[92] By its action, the Army showed that its loyalty to the government in Paris was questionable. As a result de Gaulle relieved General Challe of command in Algeria. There was a second coup attempt in April of 1961, after a January referendum in favor of independence.[93] This putsch attempt failed to gain support among an Army less passionately committed to French Algeria and was broken in only a few days.[94]

The Army's indifference towards government authority showed a lack of unity of effort between the two. With apparently little regard for the greater strategic and political consequences, the Army opted for tactical success that harmed the French efforts in the end. Examples include the bombing of the Tunisian border village Sakiet, the seizure of Ben Bella, and the widespread use of torture. One could view each of these as successes in "purely military" terms, but, in the larger view, they detracted from French goals.

Intelligence: Use of *harkis*, the SAS, and torture brought the French valuable information on insurgent activity and organization. Using this information, the French were able to bring the ALN to its knees by 1960. Operational intelligence goes beyond weapons and personnel, but in an insurgency must include character and the ways that an adversary intends to achieve his objectives. Despite 120 years of experience in Algeria, French intelligence failed to understand the depth of hostility that their policies engendered in the Muslim population. Also notable was the cultural chauvinism displayed by the French towards the Algerians. This cultural bigotry led France to misidentify the source of the insurrection as external since "principled opposition to the universal values of French civilization was, by definition, impossible".[95]

French Will: At the outbreak of hostilities in 1954, the French government was firmly behind the policy of a French Algeria, although the general public did not appear overly concerned.[96] Beginning in 1957, the issue of torture nourished the growth of an anti-war faction within France, although the idea of an independent Algeria was "unthinkable and unmentionable".[97] The steadily increasing dependence upon conscripts inevitably focused the attention of the conscripts' families on events in Algeria.

The critical point came with the rise of de Gaulle whose mandate was to resolve the crisis. De Gaulle used a carrot-and-stick approach to push for peace. The plan was comprised of renewed military operations, electoral reforms, an offer of amnesty to insurgents, and an economic development plan for Algeria.[98] The military offensive applied operational lessons from Indochina: operational fires (the Morice Line and a naval blockade) isolated the battlefield; regroupment and the SAS separated the insurgents from the people; and sequenced tactical actions drove the ALN from west to east against the Morice Line.[99] In the end, despite some success at pacification, the campaign failed to translate into political success.[100]

De Gaulle realized that the passions ignited by the war threatened to damage the Army and French society.[101] Furthermore, the ALN had become a hydra-headed monster that the French could locally suppress, but would reappear phoenix-like to menace elsewhere. In order to avoid revolution at home and escape the cost of maintaining nearly a half-million troops in Algeria, France would have to negotiate with the FLN or simply withdraw. *Colon* terror and Army insubordination only hardened de Gaulle's determination to extricate France from Algeria. Finally, it became evident that the French people cared more about their conscript loved ones than Algeria.[102]

Conclusion

Because of an unbalanced approach to combating the insurgency "the French Army could not gain the confidence of enough Algerians to counteract the effect of the elusive terrorist".[103] By failing to understand the nature of the war and focusing on tactical success, the French opened their centers of gravity to attack. The Algerians, with a better understanding of the war's nature, were able to focus their efforts on attacking French will and the legitimacy of the colonial government.

For the French, determining when they had achieved their goal of stability and order was difficult. An asymmetric moral scrutiny applied to the French meant that the FLN exploited every failure or violent excess for maximum propaganda benefit while the FLN was able to use terror without facing such condemnation. Ultimately the French will collapsed under the weight of concerns over excesses of violence, political isolation, and the inability to understand an enemy who would not admit defeat despite suffering repeated losses.

Recommendations

What can be learned from this? In insurgencies, understanding the motives of one's opponent is essential to understanding the nature of the war and determining his centers of gravity. In low intensity combat, these centers of gravity may not be subject to direct attack, especially at the strategic level. This necessitates the development of a comprehensive and coordinated response involving non-military instruments of power and will likely include politically unpopular concessions or reforms. If these reforms can ameliorate whatever societal discontent inspires the masses, it will be possible to separate them from the insurgency's more radicalized elite, which the military or law enforcement can neutralize.

Tactical and operational success can backfire if the level of violence or collateral damage is excessive. Intelligence and the precise use of force are essential to limit the consequences of military action to deserving targets. In order to win the larger political struggle the forces of order may need to take more casualties than they inflict. Cultural sensitivity is extremely important and host nation pride must be maintained. The use of foreign area specialists such as Special Forces, cognizant of local sensitivities, should be maximized. If the use of conventional troops is required, they should be trained on local customs and rituals. Combined operations with host nation forces will also help to cross the chasm of misunderstanding.

Finally, insurgencies can be won on the battlefield and lost in the public eye. Unity of effort is essential to ensure that each action is undertaken with the desired end state in mind. Linked with an aggressive information operations, adherence to unity of effort can deny an opponent exploitable propaganda opportunities while allowing the forces of order to maximize their victories.

Notes

[1] Anthony Clayton, *The Wars of French Decolonization* (New York: Longman Group UK Limited 1994), 3.

[2] Ian Beckett and John Pimlott. *Armed Forces and Modern Counter-Insurgency* (New York: St. Martin's Press Inc. 1985), 60.

[3] John Ruedy, *Modern Algeria: The Origins and Development of a Nation* (Bloomington: Indiana University Press 1992), 148.

[4] Ruedy, 192.

[5] Michael T. Kaufman, "The World: Film Studies; What Does the Pentagon See in 'Battle of Algiers,'?" *New York Times*, 7 September 2003. News/Wires. Lexis-Nexis. New York (16 December 2003).

[6] Mahfoud Bennoune, *The Making of Contemporary Algeria, 1830-1987* (New York: Press Syndicate of the University of Cambridge 1988), 29.

[7] Ibid.

[8] Ruedy, 45.

[9] Ibid., 46.

[10] Ibid., 48.

[11] Ibid., 48-49.

[12] Ibid., 49.

[13] Bennoune, 36.

[14] Ruedy, 68.

[15] Edgar O'Ballance, *The Algerian Insurrection, 1954-1962* (Hamden, CT: Archon Books 1967), 22.

[16] Alistair Horne, *A Savage War of Peace,* 2nd ed. (New York: Viking Penguin Inc. 1987), 51.

[17] Ibid., 51.

[18] Ruedy, 121.

[19] O'Ballance, 25.

[20] Horne, 62.

[21] O'Ballance, 25.

[22] Horne, 51.

[23] O'Ballance, 19.

[24] Horne, 49.

[25] O'Ballance, 19.

[26] Horne, 50.

[27] Matthew Connelly, *A Diplomatic Revolution* (New York: Oxford University Press 2002), 18.

[28] Helen Metz ed., *Algeria a Country Study,* 5th ed. (Department of the Army 1994), 87.

[29] O'Ballance, 24.

[30] Horne, 63.

[31] Alf Heggoy, A. *Insurgency and Counterinsurgency in Algeria* (Bloomington, IN: Indiana University Press 1972) 4.

[32] Clayton, 109.

[33] Metz, 37.

[34] Ruedy, 134.

[35] Horne, 40-41.

[36] Metz, 37.

[37] Heggoy, 74.

[38] John Talbott, *The War Without a Name* (New York: Alfred A. Knopf, Inc. 1980), 10.

[39] Ibid., 7.

[40] Heggoy, 6.

[41] Ibid., 7.

[42] Ibid.

[43] Metz, 34.

[44] Ruedy, 126.

[45] Ibid.

[46] Metz, 40.

[47] Ibid.

[48] Clayton, 110-111.

[49] Ibid.

[50] Metz, 44.

[51] Ibid.

[52] Heggoy, 70.

[53] Mendes-France as quoted in Horne, 98.

[54] Horne, 99.

[55] Ibid., 100.

[56] Michael Webber, "Algerian War Reading". *Nationalism and Citizenship.* <http://www.usfca.edu/fac-staff/webberm/algeria.htm#ch4>

[57] Ibid.

[58] Ruedy, 162.

[59] Webber.

[60] Ibid.

[61] Ruedy, 163.

[62] Ibid.

[63] Clayton, 121.

[64] Ibid.

[65] Heggoy, 191.

[66] Clayton, 119.

[67] Webber.

[68] Horne, 144.

[69] Heggoy, 168.

[70] Webber.

[71] Heggoy, 169.

[72] O'Ballance, 77.

[73] Ruedy, 168.

[74] Webber.

[75] Horne, 192.

[76] Ibid., 190.

[77] Ibid., 217-218.

[78] Ibid., 130.

[79] O'Ballance, 123.

[80] Ruedy, 173.

[81] Horne, 392.

[82] Connelly, 114.

[83] Clayton, 124.

[84] Heggoy, 160.

[85] Talbott, 70.

[86] Horne, 202.

[87] Ibid., 234.

[88] Clayton, 140.

[89] Horne, 277.

[90] Ibid., 282.

[91] Ruedy, 172.

[92] Connelly, 222.

[93] O'Ballance, 207.

[94] Ibid., 210.

[95] Christopher Andrew as quoted in Connelly, 70.

[96] Horne, 98.

[97] Ibid., 234.

[98] Ibid., 304-306.

[99] Clayton , 159-160.

[100] Horne, 340.

[101] Clayton, 164.

[102] O'Ballance, 183.

[103] Heggoy, 261.

Bibliography

Beckett, Ian F.W. and John Pimlott. *Armed Forces and Modern Counter-Insurgency.* New York: St. Martin's Press Inc., 1985.

Bennoune, Mahfoud. The *Making of Contemporary Algeria, 1830-1987.* New York: Press Syndicate of the University of Cambridge, 1988

Clark, Michael K. *Algeria in Turmoil.* New York: Frederick A. Praeger, 1959.

Clayton, Anthony. *The Wars of French Decolonization.* New York: Longman Group UK Limited, 1994.

Confer, Vincent. *France and Algeria: The Problem of Civil and Political Reform, 1870-1920.* Syracuse: Syracuse University Press, 1967.

Collins, Thomas. "An Analysis of the Algerian Insurrection," *Monograph on National Security Affairs,* Providence: Brown University, 1975.

Connelly, Matthew J. *A Diplomatic Revolution.* New York: Oxford University Press, 2002.

Heggoy, Alf A. *Insurgency and Counterinsurgency in Algeria.* Bloomington, IN: Indiana University Press, 1972

Horne, Alistair. *A Savage War of Peace,* 2nd ed. New York: Viking Penguin Inc. 1987.

Metz, Helen. ed. *Algeria a Country Study,* 5th ed. Department of the Army, 1994.

O'Ballance, Edgar. *The Algerian Insurrection, 1954-1962.* Hamden, CT: Archon Books, 1967.

Paret, Peter. *French Revolutionary Warfare from Indochina to Algeria.* London: Pall Mall Press Limited, 1964.

Ruedy, John D. *Modern Algeria: The Origins and Development of a Nation.* Bloomington: Indiana University Press, 1992.

Talbott, John E. *The War Without a Name.* New York: Alfred A. Knopf, Inc, 1980.

Webber, Michael. "Algerian War Reading". *Nationalism and Citizenship.* <http://www.usfca.edu/fac-staff/webberm/algeria.htm#ch4> [28 December 2003]

www.ingramcontent.com/pod-product-compliance
Lightning Source LLC
Chambersburg PA
CBHW081432310526
45790CB00020B/3732